Daksha's Gourmet Spices

Cookbook I

Happy Cooking!

Daksha Narsing
www.spicesgourmet.com

Daksha's Gourmet Spices

ISBN 0-9681253-1-X

Written by Daksha Narsing
Cover Design by Amesh Narsing
Photography by Tracey Kusiewicz

Distributed by
Daksha's Gourmet Spices
Williams Lake, B.C., Canada
V2G 3T9

Daksha's spices and cookware may be purchased at: **www.spicesgourmet.com**
E-mail: daksha@telus.net

Published by APS Publishers
Printed in Canada by Friesens

Daksha's Gourmet Spices

To Bhaskar

Preface

The inspiration for creating this unique gourmet cookbook, came from the support and encouragement of my family, friends and the many students who participated in my cooking classes.

Creating these recipes has been a "happy" and fun-filled experience in my "happy kitchen". I recall my mother always saying, being happy while cooking, produces great dishes!

This book is created to compliment the spices I blend and sell, which will make it easy for anyone to prepare delicious gourmet dishes. Many hours go into cleaning, preparing and blending these gourmet spices, such as garam masala, thana jeeroo, tea masala etc..

Happy Cooking!

Daksha Narsing

Acknowledgments

To my husband Bhaskar and children Amesh, Pravin and Sarena, for all their support, encouragement and love.

To my mother-in-law Lily Narsing, who helped me refine the art of blending spices and cooking.

To my dear friend Jasminder Hothi, for her support and contribution of the "Raas Malai" recipe, included in this book.

I am very grateful to Helen Noonan and Nancy Leach Schaeffer for their time and effort put into editing my first cookbook.

Last but not least I am very grateful to all of my family members and friends for their love and encouragement.

How to Use This Book

This cookbook compliments the spices that are blended by Daksha's Gourmet Spices.

Prepare ginger/garlic masala (page 72), green chillie masala (page 72) and garlic masala (page 72). These are fresh mixtures and can be made in advance and stored in the freezer.

Ginger/garlic masala and green chillie masala are used in many of the recipes in this cookbook. Garlic masala is used for fish dishes.

Spicy Appetizer Dishes

SPICY TEA (CHAI)

Serves four

INGREDIENTS

3 cups of water
1 inch cube ginger (sliced)
2 tea bags (regular or
decaffeinated.)
½ teaspoon tea masala
1 cup milk
sugar to taste

METHOD

1 Heat in a pan 3 cups of water, tea bags, sliced ginger and tea masala, on medium heat.
2 Let mixture come to a boil and add 1 cup of milk.
3 Allow the mixture to come to a boil and remove from heat. Strain in tea pot and serve.
4 Add sugar if required, when serving (to individual taste).

SPICY MEAT BALLS

Serves six to eight

INGREDIENTS

2 lbs of ground meat (chicken, beef or lamb)
4 teaspoons ginger/garlic masala
1 teaspoon green chillie masala
2 teaspoons garam masala
2 teaspoons thana jeeroo
½ teaspoon red chillie powder
½ teaspoon turmeric powder
1½ teaspoon salt
2 medium onions (minced)
8 tablespoons of olive oil
2 cassia sticks (cinnamon bark)
1 whole cardamom
2 cloves
6 peppercorns
1 tablespoon chopped cilantro
1 tablespoon cider vinegar
½ cup of warm water

METHOD

1 Mix all the spices with 3 tablespoons of oil to make a paste. Thoroughly blend the paste with the ground meat.

2 Allow meat to marinate for at least two hours in the refrigerator.

3 Grate two medium onions. Squeeze grated onions to remove excess onion water and blend with ground meat. Finely chop cilantro and add to meat.

4 In a heated frying pan pour 6 tablespoons of oil and add the whole cassia sticks, cardamom, cloves and peppercorns. Sauté to flavor the oil.

5 In a separate bowl, mix vinegar with the warm water. Use to dampen fingers before shaping the meat balls.

6 Make the meat balls into 1 to 2 inch rounds. Place them in the heated pan on medium heat with the whole spices.

7 Cover and allow to cook for 5 minutes before stirring. Once all the sides are brown continue to stir occasionally, so that they cook thoroughly without burning.

Serve with spicy tomato sauce.

SAMOSAS

Samosas is one of India's delicacy dish. They are made from a light pastry filled with spicy meat or vegetables and freeze very well.

INGREDIENTS FOR MEAT FILLING

3 lbs of ground meat
1 medium onion chopped
4 teaspoons ginger/garlic masala
1 teaspoon green chillie masala
3 teaspoons garam masala
3 teaspoons thana jeeroo
2 teaspoons red chillie powder
1 teaspoon turmeric powder
3 teaspoons salt
¾ cup olive oil
3 cassia sticks (cinnamon bark)
2 cardamoms
4 cloves
8 peppercorns
2 tablespoons of chopped cilantro

METHOD

1 Mix all the spices in 4 tablespoons of oil.
2 Add mixture to ground meat and blend well.
3 Heat 5 tablespoons of oil in a pan. Add whole spices to flavor oil.
4 Add spiced ground meat and stir until meat is browned. Allow to cook on low heat until oil separates and meat is thoroughly cooked.
5 Sauté onions in a separate pan in 4 tablespoons of oil, till golden brown.
6 Add onions and chopped cilantro to cooked ground meat and stir. Set aside to cool.

INGREDIENTS FOR VEGETABLE FILLING

5 or 6 medium potatoes chopped
1 medium onion chopped
1 cup peas (frozen or fresh)
2 teaspoons ginger/garlic masala
1 teaspoon green chillie masala
1 teaspoon red chillie powder
2 teaspoons thana jeeroo
½ teaspoon turmeric powder
2 teaspoons salt
5 tablespoons olive oil
2 tablespoons chopped cilantro

METHOD

1 In a pan heat oil and add whole cumin seeds.
2 Add chopped onions and sauté.
3 Add chopped potatoes and peas plus remaining spices and stir.
4 Cover and allow to cook on low heat till vegetables are cooked.
5 Garnish with chopped cilantro.

Samosas Cont..

Pastry

4 cups of all purpose flour
1 teaspoon salt
2 tablespoons corn oil
2 to 3 cups of cold water

Mix salt and oil in the flour and bind with ice water. Knead till the dough is workable.

Making the Pastry

Make one inch balls with dough and roll out to a 2 inch round. Spread some oil and sprinkle with flour. Join two 2 inch rounds together and flour both sides again then roll out to about a 6 to 8 inch round. Cook on a tava* or a non-stick frying pan. Cook lightly on one side and lightly on the other. Separate the two pastries gently by hand. Place on a large towel covering the pastries so as not to let them dry out. Once the pastries are all made, cut them in 3 inch strips.

Paste

Take about 4 tablespoons of flour and add cold water and stir till the mixture is a pasty consistency.

SAMOSAS CONT..

Filling the Samosas

Fold pastry in a triangular shape, leaving a flap at one end of the triangle free. Using paste stick the flaps of pastry together, leaving the free flap open to fill pastry with the fillings (meat or vegetable fillings). Fill the triangle with filling and close the flap using more paste, making a triangular samosa. Place samosas on a tray and cover with a clean towel. Samosas can be placed in an airtight container and placed in a freezer for later use

Frying the Samosas

In a deep fryer place about 4 cups of oil, on medium heat. Place samosas in the hot oil and fry till golden brown.

*a Tava is an Indian pan used to prepare many of the Indian breads such as roti and naan. One can use a non-stick frying pan.

MOOTHYA (SPICY PATTIES)

Serves four to six

INGREDIENTS

2 cups of cooked rice
1 medium potato grated
1 medium onion chopped
1 cup zucchini grated
6 tablespoons chana flour
1 teaspoon ginger/garlic masala
1 teaspoon red chillie powder
1 teaspoon thana jeeroo
1 teaspoon salt
¼ teaspoon turmeric powder
8 tablespoons corn oil
1 teaspoon fruit salt*
¼ cup warm water

*Can be substituted with baking powder

METHOD

1   Mix all the vegetables, rice, chana flour and spices (except fruit salt) with warm water in a bowl.

2   Add fruit salt to dough and blend in.

3   Make 2 inch round patties about half an inch thick. Place patties on a hot frying pan on medium heat with 8 tablespoons of oil.

4   Cook patties on both sides till golden brown.

Various kinds of vegetables could be used, such as leftover corn, carrots, beans, peas etc..

VADAS

INGREDIENTS

¼ cup Dokra mix (see Dokra)
¼ cup cream of wheat
2 tablespoons corn meal
1 tablespoon rice flour
1 tablespoon all purpose flour
4 tablespoons plain yogurt
1 tablespoon sour cream
1 teaspoon ginger/garlic masala
1 teaspoon green chillie masala
1 teaspoon salt
1 teaspoon fruit salt*
2 tablespoons chopped cilantro
¼ cup warm water
4 cups of corn oil

*Can be substituted with baking powder

METHOD

1 Mix all the ingredients (except fruit salt and oil) in a bowl with warm water, making mixture the consistency of a pancake mix.
2 Add fruit salt to mixture just before frying.
3 In a deep fryer heat about 4 cups of oil on medium heat.
4 Drop small half inch balls of dough in the hot oil and fry to a crispy golden brown.

Vadas make a great party snack!

PATARYA (SPICY SPINACH ROLLS)

Serves six to eight

INGREDIENTS

1 cup chana flour
½ cup corn flour
3 tablespoons rice flour
3 tablespoons all purpose flour
2 teaspoons grated ginger
2 teaspoons red chillie powder
2 teaspoons garam masala
2 teaspoons salt
2 teaspoons sugar
juice of ½ a lemon
2 tablespoons sesame seeds
¼ cup of oil
½ cup of water
2 bunches of spinach leaves or
2 dozen large size spinach leaves

METHOD

1 Wash and dry upto 2 dozen large spinach leaves and set aside.
2 Mix the rest of the ingredients in a bowl to make a paste (except oil).
3 Spread paste on dry spinach leaves and fold and roll (like cabbage rolls).
4 Heat ¼ cup of oil in a frying pan on medium heat. Place spinach rolls in hot oil and turn frequently until rolls are cooked and crispy on the outside.

Spinach can be substituted with Taro Leaves.
Spinach rolls go well with spicy tea.

POTATO SNACKS

INGREDIENTS

4 large potatoes
3 cups of chana flour
3 teaspoons red chillie powder
4 teaspoons salt
3 tablespoons corn oil
juice of ½ a lemon
4 cups of corn oil

METHOD

1 Boil potatoes till cooked. Mash potatoes to a smooth consistency.
2 Add the rest of the ingredients (except 4 cups of oil) to potatoes to make a soft dough.
3 Heat 4 cups of oil in a deep fryer on medium heat.
4 Put dough through a ricer, over hot oil and fry till golden brown.
5 Remove and place in a colander. Store in closed jar when cooled.

A great party snack!

BHAJYAS (PAKODAS)

Serves eight

INGREDIENTS

6 tablespoons of chana flour
2 tablespoons of all purpose flour
2 teaspoon ginger/garlic masala
1 teaspoon green chillie masala
¼ teaspoon turmeric powder
½ teaspoon red chillie powder
1½ teaspoons garam masala
2 teaspoons salt
2 tablespoons corn oil
2 cups of water
1 cup finely chopped spinach
1 medium size potato grated
1 medium size onion grated
1 cup grated zucchini
4 cups of corn oil
1 teaspoon fruit salt*

*can be substituted with baking powder

METHOD

1   Mix all the spices and flours with 2 tablespoons of oil and water in a bowl. Make a mixture to a consistency of a pancake mix.

2   Add the grated potato, onion, zucchini and chopped spinach to the dough and stir. Add fruit salt just before frying and mix.

3   Heat about 4 cups of corn oil in a deep fryer on medium heat. Carefully drop about a tablespoon of the mixture by hand in the heated oil. Allow the pakodas to cook until golden brown and remove from oil.

DOKRA (STEAMED LENTIL CAKE)

Serves six to eight

DOKRA MIX INGREDIENTS
3 cups of rice
1 ½ cups of chana daal
¾ cup urad daal

DOKRA INGREDIENTS

3 ¾ cups of Dokra mix
500g tub of plain yogurt
2 teaspoons salt
1 teaspoon green chillie masala
2 teaspoons grated ginger
1 teaspoon fruit salt
1 cup warm water
½ cup of corn oil
2 tablespoons black mustard seeds
4 tablespoons sesame seeds
4 tablespoons chopped cilantro

A great party snack!

METHOD
Dokra Mixture
1 Grind all the daals in a coffee grinder.
2 Sieve the mixture to obtain a grainy texture.

METHOD
1 Mix together in a bowl dokra mix, yogurt, green chillies, ginger, salt and warm water.
2 Let mixture stand for about 4 to 6 hours at room temperature.
3 Add fruit salt to the mixture just before pouring into greased pans (9 inch cake pans).
4 Sprinkle sesame seeds on top of the mixture.
5 Place pans on a steamer tray, in a pot with about an inch of water at the bottom of pot.
6 Steam for about 30 minutes on medium heat or till fully cooked.
7 Cut Dokra into squares when cooled. In a small pan heat 3 tablespoons of oil. Add black mustard seeds and allow to pop.
8 Sprinkle the oil and seeds over Dokra and garnish with chopped cilantro.

PAN ROASTED POTATOES

Serves four

INGREDIENTS

4 large potatoes
½ teaspoon turmeric powder
1 teaspoon salt
6 tablespoons olive oil

METHOD

1 Wash and cut peeled potatoes in quarters. Add turmeric and salt on cut up potatoes.
2 Heat oil in a frying pan and add potatoes with salt and turmeric.
3 Cook covered on medium heat, stirring occasionally for about 20 minutes.
4 Remove lid and cook on low heat turning potatoes until they are cooked and golden brown.

This makes a great side dish!

MEASUREMENTS

Volume Measurement

¼ teaspoon = 1.2 ml
½ teaspoon = 2.5 ml
1 teaspoon = 5.0 ml
1 tablespoon = 15 ml

¼ cup = 60 ml
½ cup = 125 ml
¾ cup = 180 ml
1 cup = 250 ml

Weight Conversion

1oz = 28 grams
6oz = 168 grams

¼ lb = 112 grams
½ lb = 225 grams
1 lb = 450 grams

Spicy Meat, Poultry & Fish Dishes

Notes

CHICKEN PILAF

Serves six to eight

INGREDIENTS
3 lbs chicken cubed and cleaned
3 teaspoons ginger/garlic masala
1 teaspoon green chillie masala
2 teaspoons garam masala
2 teaspoons thana jeeroo
1 teaspoon red chillie powder
¼ teaspoon turmeric powder
1 ½ teaspoon salt
2 cassia sticks
2 cardamoms
4 cloves
10 tablespoons of olive oil
2 tablespoons chopped cilantro

RICE INGREDIENTS
2 cups of basmati rice
2 teaspoons salt
2 cups of water

Note: Beef or lamb can be substituted for chicken.

Serve with spicy tomato sauce.

METHOD
1 Mix all the spices with 4 tablespoons of oil to make a paste. Thoroughly blend the paste with the chicken.

2 Allow meat to marinate for 2 hours in the refrigerator.

3 Wash 2 cups of rice and cook in a deep pan with 2 cups of water and 2 teaspoon salt.

4 In the meantime, heat 6 tablespoons of oil in a deep pan. Add cassia sticks, cardamoms and cloves. Sauté to flavor the oil.

5 Add chicken and stir. Allow to cook on medium heat for about 15 minutes. Cover and stir occasionally, until meat is half cooked.

6 Allow rice to half cook on medium to low heat for about 10 to 15 minutes. Remove from stove and drain off water in a sieve.

7 Place half cooked rice on top of meat covering meat completely.

8 Add ½ cup of water and cook covered on low heat till both the rice and the meat is cooked thoroughly. Cook for approximately 30 minutes.

Serve on a large platter and garnish with chopped cilantro.

CHICKEN CURRY

Serves eight to ten

INGREDIENTS

3 lbs of chicken, cleaned and cubed
4 teaspoons ginger/garlic masala
1 teaspoon green chillie masala
2 teaspoons garam masala
2 teaspoons thana jeeroo
1 teaspoon red chillie powder
¼ teaspoon turmeric powder
1½ teaspoon salt
3 medium tomatoes diced
1 medium onion chopped
2 tablespoons tomato paste
8 tablespoons of olive oil
2 cassia sticks
2 cardamoms
4 cloves
6 black peppercorns
2 tablespoons chopped cilantro

METHOD

1 Mix all the spices with 3 tablespoons of oil to make a paste. Thoroughly blend the spices with the chicken and allow to marinate for 2 hours in the refrigerator, before cooking.

2 Heat 5 tablespoons of oil in a pan and add cassia sticks, cardamoms, cloves and peppercorns to flavor the oil. Add chopped onions and sauté till lightly brown.

3 Add marinated chicken cubes and stir. Cover and cook, stirring occasionally, on medium heat for approx. 20 minutes.

4 Mix tomato paste in about 1 cup of water and add to curry . Dice 2 tomatoes fine and add to the curry.

5 Cook covered on medium heat for 30 - 40 minutes until curry is nice and thick and chicken is thoroughly cooked.

6 Transfer to a heated serving dish and garnish with chopped cilantro.

Serve hot over a bed of rice or with roti, naan (pita bread), foolecha or dinner rolls.

BHABUTI

Serves eight to ten

INGREDIENTS
1 lb of ground beef
2 teaspoons ginger/garlic masala
½ teaspoon green chillie masala
2 teaspoons garam masala
2 teaspoons thana jeeroo
½ teaspoon red chillie powder
½ teaspoon turmeric powder
2 teaspoons salt
8 tablespoons oil
2 cassia sticks
2 cardamoms
4 cloves
6 black peppercorns
2 tablespoons of chopped cilantro

INGREDIENTS FOR BAKING

1 bunch of green onions chopped
1½ cups of bread crumbs
2 eggs beaten
2 cups peas (frozen or fresh)
3 carrots chopped
2 cups of boiled potatoes - cubed
2 cups of cooked rice
½ cup of water
cooked ground meat

METHOD
1 Mix all the spices with 3 tablespoons of oil to make a paste.
2 Blend spice paste thoroughly in the ground meat.
3 In a pan heat 5 tablespoons of oil, on medium heat. Add cassia sticks, cardamoms, cloves and peppercorns to flavor the oil.
4 Add ground meat (it is not necessary to marinate the meat for 2 hours in the refrigerator as most other recipes) and stir, till meat is browned and cooked.

METHOD
1 Mix all the ingredients for baking, in a covered casserole dish. Bake at 350°F for one hour.
2 Garnish with chopped cilantro

Great dish to make with leftovers.

SPICY FRIED FISH

Serves four to six

INGREDIENTS

1½ lbs of fish (cod, snapper, sole or salmon)
2 teaspoons garlic masala
½ teaspoon green chillie masala
1½ teaspoons thana jeeroo
2 teaspoons crushed cumin
½ teaspoon red chillie powder
¼ teaspoon turmeric powder
1 teaspoon salt
8 tablespoons olive oil
½ cup of all purpose flour
2 tablespoons chopped cilantro

METHOD

1 Wash fillet fish and cut into 2 inches by 4 inches strips (approximately) or cut into ¾ inch fish steaks.

2 Make an oil and spice paste by combining 2 tablespoons of oil and all the spices listed.

3 Coat the fish strips with spice paste and marinate in refrigerator for 2 hours or more.

4 When ready to cook, heat 6 tablespoons of oil in a frying pan.

5 Coat the fish lightly with flour and fry , turning occasionally on medium heat, until golden brown.

6 Transfer to a warm platter. Garnish with chopped cilantro and serve immediately.

SHRIMP CURRY

Serves 4 to six

INGREDIENTS

1 lb cooked shrimp
1 teaspoon garlic masala
½ teaspoon green chillie masala
1 teaspoon thana jeeroo
2 teaspoon crushed cumin
½ teaspoon red chillie powder
¼ teaspoon turmeric powder
1 teaspoon salt
1 cup chopped green onions
1 medium tomato diced
2 tablespoons tomato paste
6 tablespoons of olive oil
½ cup of water

METHOD

1   In a pan heat 6 tablespoons of oil. Sauté finely chopped onions.
2   Add the spices listed and stir.
3   Add shrimps and stir.
4   Mix ½ cup of water and 2 tablespoons of tomato paste and add to shrimp and stir. Add finely chopped tomatoes. Cover and allow to cook for about 20 minutes on medium heat, till shrimps are cooked.

Serve over rice or noodles.

SPICY ROASTED CHICKEN

Serves six to eight

INGREDIENTS

3 lbs of whole chicken (or pieces)
4 teaspoons ginger/garlic masala
1 teaspoon green chillie masala
2 teaspoons garam masala
2 teaspoons thana jeeroo
1 teaspoon red chillie powder
½ teaspoon turmeric powder
1½ teaspoon salt
4 tablespoons olive oil
5 medium potatoes cut in four
4 carrots chopped
1 large onion cut in four
1 whole onion

Preheat oven to 375ºF

Serve with Spicy tomato sauce or cilantro chutney.

METHOD

1 Mix all spices with the oil and tomato paste.
2 Coat the chicken thoroughly with spice paste, being sure to coat the inside cavity of the chicken.
3 Allow the chicken to marinate for 2 hours in the refrigerator.
4 Place a peeled onion in the cavity of the chicken and place in a covered roasting pan. Place washed, peeled and cut up vegetables listed, around the chicken and cover.
5 Place roast in a preheated oven of 375ºF and cook for about one hour, till vegetables and chicken is thoroughly cooked. Baste chicken and vegetables occasionally.
6 Remove the lid of the roasting pan and continue to cook for another 10 minutes to brown the chicken.

TANDOORI CHICKEN

Serves eight to ten

INGREDIENTS

3 lbs of chicken pieces
3 teaspoons ginger/garlic masala
2 teaspoons tandoori paste or powder
2 teaspoons garam masala
2 teaspoons thana jeeroo
½ teaspoon red chillie powder
½ teaspoon turmeric powder
1½ teaspoons salt
1 cup yogurt
2 tablespoons chopped cilantro

Preheat oven 350ºF

METHOD

1 Clean chicken pieces and remove skin.
2 Mix together the listed spices with one cup of yogurt.
3 Marinate the chicken for 3 hours or more in a refrigerator.
4 Preheat oven to 350ºF. Place chicken in covered casserole dish and cook for one hour, till chicken is fully cooked.
5 Remove lid and cook for another 10 to 15 minutes.
6 Remove cooked chicken and place on a warm serving platter. Spread the remaining sauce around the chicken. Garnish with chopped cilantro and serve immediately.

Serve with basmati rice, roti or naan.

Notes

Spicy Barbecues

Notes

Barbecued Salmon In Lettuce Leaf

Serves four to six

INGREDIENTS

1 salmon cut in 1 inch steaks
2 teaspoons garlic masala
½ teaspoon green chillie masala
2 teaspoons thana jeeroo
2 teaspoons ground cumin
½ teaspoon red chillie powder
¼ teaspoon turmeric powder
1 teaspoon salt
3 tablespoons olive oil
6 to 7 lettuce leaves

METHOD

1 Mix spices with oil to make a paste.
2 Spread fish with the paste and marinate for one hour in the refrigerator.
3 Carefully remove lettuce leaves making sure they are intact. Roll lettuce leaf with a rolling pin. This makes the leaf more pliable to work with.
4 Place marinated fish on lettuce leaf and fold over fish, closing leaf with a toothpick. Make sure both sides of the fish steak is covered.
5 Barbecue the fish in lettuce leaf on medium heat for approximately 5 to 10 minutes each side or until fish is cooked.
6 Serve with cilantro chutney

Note: Corn on the cob, salad and naan (or pita bread) make tasty additions to this meal.

BARBECUED CHICKEN KABOBS

Serves six to eight

INGREDIENTS

3 lbs of cubed chicken
3 teaspoons ginger/garlic masala
½ teaspoon green chillie masala
2 teaspoons garam masala
2 teaspoons thana jeeroo
1 teaspoon red chillie powder
1 teaspoon turmeric powder
2 teaspoons salt
3 tablespoons olive oil
2 small zucchinis cut in 1" cubes
2 cups of mushrooms (whole)
1 cup of cherry tomatoes
1 green pepper cut in 1" squares

Serve with spicy tomato sauce or cilantro chutney.

METHOD

1 Mix spices with oil to make a paste.

2 Spread the paste thoroughly over chicken and marinate for two hours in the refrigerator.

3 Wash and cut zucchinis and green pepper in 1" squares. Wash and drain mushrooms and cherry tomatoes.

4 While the chicken is marinating prepare wooden skewers by soaking them in cold water for at least 30 minutes. (This reduces the chance of the skewers burning on the barbecue). Heat the barbecue on medium heat.

5 Arrange on skewers marinated chicken and vegetables.

6 Cook kabobs on barbecue for approximately 20 minutes turning frequently or until chicken is thoroughly cooked.

BARBECUED MEAT BALLS

Serves six to eight

INGREDIENTS

2 lbs of ground meat (chicken, beef or lamb)

4 teaspoons ginger/garlic masala

1 teaspoon green chillie masala

2 teaspoons thana jeeroo

2 teaspoons garam masala

½ teaspoon red chillie powder

½ teaspoon turmeric powder

1½ teaspoons salt

1 large onion

4 tablespoons of olive oil

1 tablespoon chopped cilantro

1 tablespoon cider vinegar

½ cup of warm water

Serve with spicy tomato sauce or cilantro chutney.

METHOD

1 Mix all the spices with the oil to make a paste. Thoroughly blend the paste with the ground meat.

2 Allow the meat/spice mixture to marinate for 2 hours in the refrigerator.

3 While meat is marinating soak wooden skewers in cold water for at least half an hour.

4 Grate 1 large onion. Squeeze grated onions to remove excess onion water and blend with ground meat. Add chopped cilantro now.

5 Mix cider vinegar with warm water. Use to dampen fingers before shaping the meat balls.

6 Arrange meat balls on skewers and barbecue on medium heat, turning frequently until meat is thoroughly cooked.

BARBECUED SPICY ROAST CHICKEN

Serves four

INGREDIENTS

1 whole chicken (washed)
3 teaspoons ginger/garlic masala
1 teaspoon green chillie masala
2 teaspoons garam masala
2 teaspoons thana jeeroo
1 teaspoon red chillie powder
1 teaspoon turmeric powder
2 teaspoons salt
4 tablespoons olive oil
1 whole onion peeled

METHOD

1   Marinate the whole chicken with the paste of mixed spices for 2 hours in the refrigerator.

2   Place a whole onion inside the cavity of the chicken.

3   Heat barbecue on low heat and place whole chicken on the top shelf.

4   Place aluminum pie plates with water on the bottom shelf

5   Cover barbecue and allow to cook on low heat for about an hour, making sure that the plates always have water, while cooking.

End result is a golden, crispy moist chicken.

SPICY BARBECUED CHICKEN PIECES

Serves four to six

3 lbs of chicken breast cut in big pieces with back attached. Wash and drain meat before applying the marinade.

Using the same marinate as the barbecued roast chicken (page 38), marinate the chicken pieces with the spice paste two hours before cooking, in a refrigerator.

Heat barbecue on medium heat and place the chicken on the grill of the barbecue. Turn the chicken frequently so as not to burn the meat. Cook until chicken is thoroughly cooked.

Serve with spicy tomato sauce or cilantro chutney.

Note: The marinated chicken can be kept in a freezer in freezer bags and use when needed. A great way of having spicy barbecues when camping.

Notes

Spicy Vegetable Dishes

Notes

EGGPLANT AND POTATO CURRY

Serves four

INGREDIENTS

1 eggplant cut in chunks
1 large potato cut in chunks
1 medium onion chopped finely
1 large tomato diced
1 teaspoon ginger/garlic masala
½ teaspoon green chillie masala
2 teaspoons thana jeeroo
½ teaspoon red chillie powder
¼ teaspoon tumeric powder
1 teaspoon salt
2 tablespoons chopped cilantro
6 tablespoons of olive oil
2 teaspoons whole cumin seeds
¼ cup water

METHOD

1 Heat 6 tablespoons of oil in a saucepan on medium heat. Add whole cumin seeds and chopped onions. Sauté until onions are golden brown.

2 Mix rest of the spices with cut up potato and add to the onions.

3 Cover and cook on medium heat for about 20 minutes stirring frequently. When potatoes are partially cooked add the eggplant and ¼ cup of water.

4 Allow to cook on low heat for about 10 minutes, stirring occasionally. Add diced tomatoes, cover and cook for another 10 to 15 minutes or until all the vegetables are cooked.

5 Garnish with chopped cilantro

Serve with roti or rice.

PEAS AND POTATO CURRY

Serves four

INGREDIENTS

3 medium potatoes
1 cup peas (frozen or fresh)
1 medium onion chopped
1 medium tomato diced
1 teaspoon ginger/garlic masala
½ teaspoon green chillie masala
2 teaspoons thana jeeroo
½ teaspoon red chillie powder
¼ teaspoon turmeric powder
1 teaspoon salt
2 teaspoons whole cumin seeds
1 tablespoon tomato paste
1 cup water
6 tablespoons olive oil
2 tablespoons chopped cilantro

METHOD

1 Heat 6 tablespoons of oil in a saucepan on medium heat. Add whole cumin seeds and chopped onions. Sauté until onions are golden brown.

2 Mix the rest of the spices with cut up potatoes and peas and add to the onions.

3 Cover and allow to cook for about 15 minutes or till potatoes are almost cooked.

4 Add chopped tomatoes, tomato paste and water and stir. Allow to cook another 10 to 15 minutes on medium heat stirring occasionally.

5 Garnish with chopped cilantro.

Serve with roti or rice.

SPICY CORN

Serves four

INGREDIENTS

4 cups of grated corn or 2 cans of corn

1 teaspoon ginger/garlic masala

¼ teaspoon green chillie masala

½ teaspoon red chillie powder

1 teaspoon salt

juice of ½ a lemon

½ teaspoon black mustard seeds

4 tablespoons olive oil

1 tablespoon sesame seeds

1 tablespoon chopped cilantro

METHOD

1 Heat 4 tablespoons of oil in a pan. Add black mustard seeds, allowing the seeds to pop.

2 Add ginger/garlic, green chillie masala, red chillie powder and salt to the corn, in a separate bowl.

3 Add the spiced corn to the hot oil with mustard seeds and stir. Add juice of half a lemon and stir.

4 Cover and allow to cook on medium heat for about 10 to 15 minutes.

Garnish with sesame seeds and chopped cilantro.

SPICY POTATO

Serves four

INGREDIENTS

4 cups large potatoes
2 teaspoon ginger/garlic masala
½ teaspoon green chillie masala
½ teaspoon red chillie powder
1 teaspoon thana jeeroo
½ teaspoon turmeric powder
2 teaspoon salt
1 teaspoon whole cumin seeds
1 teaspoon black mustard seeds
6 tablespoons olive oil
2 tablespoons chopped cilantro

METHOD

1 Peel and slice potatoes into thin slices. Wash sliced potatoes and allow to drain in a colander.

2 Add masalas, spices and salt to the potatoes.

3 In a frying pan heat oil on medium heat.

4 In the hot oil add whole cumin seeds and black mustard seeds and allow to pop.

5 As soon as the seeds pop add potatoes with spices and stir well. Cover and cook on low heat, stirring occasionally, until the potatoes are cooked.

Garnish with chopped cilantro.

SPICY PEPPER AND POTATO DISH

Serves four

INGREDIENTS

½ a bell pepper
2 large potatoes
1 medium tomato
1 medium onion
1 teaspoon ginger/garlic masala
½ teaspoon red chillie powder
½ teaspoon turmeric powder
1 teaspoon thana jeeroo
1 teaspoon salt
1 teaspoon cumin seeds
4 tablespoons olive oil

METHOD

1   Peel and cut potatoes into small 1 inch cubes. Chop bell pepper and onions and place in a dish.
2   Chop tomatoes and set aside.
3   Add masalas and spices to the vegetables in the dish.
4   In a frying pan or wok heat 4 tablespoons of oil on medium heat.
5   Add cumin seeds to the hot oil and allow to pop.
6   As soon as the seeds pop, add the vegetables with spices and stir.
7   Allow to cook covered for 10 minutes on medium heat stirring occasionally.
8   Add chopped tomatoes and allow to cook for a further 10 to 15 minutes on low heat until all the vegetables are cooked.

Notes

Spicy Lentil Dishes

ABOUT LENTILS

Lentils are a good source of protein. Lentils do not require as much spices as meat or vegetable dishes. These dishes are great any time of the year.

The lentils mentioned in this book are available in some of the larger supermarkets or specialty Indian grocery shops.

VADHU (SPROUTED MUNG CURRY)

Serves four to six

INGREDIENTS

1 cup mung beans
1 teaspoon ginger/garlic masala
¼ teaspoon green chillie masala
¼ red chillie powder
½ teaspoon salt
¼ teaspoon turmeric powder
2 tablespoons olive oil

Serve with roti, bread or pita bread.

METHOD

1 Soak mung beans in warm water for about 4 hours, till mung beans are twice their original size.

2 Drain and tie up mung beans in a clean white cotton cloth (cheese cloth preferably) and place in a bowl or deep dish and cover.

3 Keep mung in a warm place for approximately 24 hours. Mung beans will sprout. The shoots may even grow through the cotton cloth.

4 Remove the sprouted mung from the cloth. Wash and drain in a colander. Mung beans are ready for cooking.

5 Place mung in a pan and add ginger/garlic masala, green chillie masala, salt, turmeric, oil and finely chopped onion.

6 Cook on low heat for about 1 hour or till mung is cooked.

Urad Toower Daal

Serves four to six

INGREDIENTS

½ **cup of urad daal**
½ **cup toower daal**
1 teaspoon ginger/garlic masala
½ **teaspoon green chillie masala**
¼ **teaspoon red chillie powder**
¼ **teaspoon turmeric powder**
½ **teaspoon salt**
2 tablespoons ghee*
1 teaspoon garam masala
3 cups of water

*ghee is clarified butter.

METHOD

1 Cook both urad and toower daal with 3 cups of water in a pressure cooker for about 30 to 40 minutes on medium heat.
2 Sieve cooked daal through a fine sieve in a dish.
3 Add green chillie masala, salt and turmeric to daal and stir.
4 Heat ghee in a pan on medium heat. Add ginger/garlic masala and sauté.
5 Add daal with spices and stir. Cover and allow to cook on low heat for approximately 30 minutes.
6 Once daal comes to a boil, shut stove and garnish with a sprinkle of garam masala.

Great with roti, bread or pita bread.

MUNG DAAL

Serves four

INGREDIENTS

1 cup mung daal
1 teaspoon ginger/garlic masala
½ teaspoon green chillie masala
½ teaspoon salt
¼ teaspoon red chillie powder
½ teaspoon turmeric powder
3 tablespoons olive oil

METHOD

1 Wash and soak mung daal in warm water for about 4 hours. The daal will expand to twice it's size.

2 Wash daal and drain off water. Add spices to daal.

3 Heat about 3 tablespoons of oil in a pan. Add daal with spices, to the hot oil.

4 Pour water upto the level of the daal and cook on low heat for about 20 to 30 minutes, until daal is cooked.

Roti, bread or pita bread will go well with this dish.

MUNG CURRY

INGREDIENTS

1 cup mung beans
1 teaspoon ginger/garlic masala
½ teaspoon green chillie masala
¼ teaspoon red chillie powder
½ teaspoon turmeric powder
1 teaspoon salt
3 tablespoons olive oil
4 or 5 curry leaves (limeree leaves)
1 tomato

METHOD

1   Wash mung beans thoroughly and cook on medium heat, for approximately 30 minutes, in a deep pan with plenty of water.

2   When mung beans are half cooked add tomato cut in large chunks. Cook further 10 to 20 minutes till both tomatoes and mung is cooked.

3   Remove pan off the stove and add remaining spices to the cooked mung and stir.

4   In a separate pan heat 3 tablespoons of oil and add curry leaves, to flavor the oil.

5   Pour the mung mixture into the pan. Cover and allow to cook for about 10 to 15 minutes on low heat.

Serve with roti, bread or pita bread.

ZUCCHINI WITH CHANA DAAL

Serves four

INGREDIENTS

1 cup chana daal
1 small zucchini
1 teaspoon ginger/garlic masala
¼ teaspoon green chillie masala
½ teaspoon red chillie powder
½ teaspoon turmeric powder
½ teaspoon black mustard seeds
½ teaspoon salt
3 tablespoons olive oil
½ cup of water

METHOD

1 Soak daal in warm water for about 4 hours until daal is twice its original size.
2 Wash daal and drain off excess water and add spices.
3 Heat oil in a pan and add mustard seeds till they pop.
4 Add daal with spices into the pan and pour ½ cup of water.
5 Cover and cook on medium heat for approximately 10 to 15 minutes or until daal is half cooked.
6 Add cut up zucchini and cook covered on low heat for another 10 minutes or until both daal and zucchini is cooked.

Great with roti, bread or pita bread.

Black Eye Bean Curry

Serves six

INGREDIENTS

1 cup black eye beans
½ medium onion chopped
1 teaspoon ginger/garlic masala
½ teaspoon red chillie powder
1 teaspoon salt
¼ teaspoon turmeric powder
2 tablespoons tomato paste
½ cup of water
1 teaspoon basil
½ teaspoon oregano
1 teaspoon brown sugar
2 teaspoons Worcestershire sauce
4 tablespoons olive oil
10 to 12 ajwan seeds* (lovage)

*Ajwan seed is allied to the licorice family.

METHOD

1 Cook black eye beans in plenty of water, on medium heat for about 20 to 30 minutes, until fully cooked.

2 Drain the beans and place in dish. Add ginger/garlic masala, red chillie powder, turmeric and salt.

3 Heat oil in pan and add ajwan seeds and chopped onions and sauté.

4 Add beans with spices to the onions and stir. Stir in the tomato paste, half cup of water, basil, oregano, brown sugar and Worcestershire sauce.

5 Cover and allow to cook on low heat for about 40 to 45 minutes, stirring occasionally.

Serve with roti, bread or pita bread.

TOOWER DAAL

Serves six to eight

INGREDIENTS

1 cup toower daal
1 medium tomato
¼ teaspoon red chillie powder
¼ teaspoon salt
3 cups of water

INGREDIENTS FOR SIEVED DAAL

2 teaspoons grated ginger
½ teaspoon red chillie powder
½ teaspoon turmeric powder
1 teaspoon salt
juice of one lemon

INGREDIENTS FOR THE HOT OIL

3 tablespoons of corn oil
2 dry red chillies
½ teaspoon black mustard seeds
½ teaspoon whole cumin seeds
1 tablespoon brown sugar
2 tablespoons chopped cilantro

METHOD

1 Wash daal 3 times in warm water.
2 In a pressure cooker combine washed daal, water, salt and red chillie powder and tomato cut in chunks.
3 Cook daal until a soupy consistency, on medium heat for about 35 minutes (about an hour on regular pot).
4 Sieve daal into a dish. Add fresh grated ginger, red chillie powder, turmeric, juice of one lemon and salt and stir.
5 Heat oil in a separate pot on high heat. Add all the ingredients for hot oil and allow seeds to pop and red chillies to brown. Add the daal with spices and quickly close the lid (bringing the heat down to medium), for 30 seconds and stir.
6 Add brown sugar to daal. Cover and allow to cook for about 5 to 10 minutes until daal comes to boil. Garnish with cilantro.

Serve daal on a bed of rice.

Notes

Indian Breads

Notes

CHAPPATI OR ROTI

ROTI IS AN "INDIAN BREAD" AND COMPLIMENTS ALL CURRY DISHES.

INGREDIENTS

1 cup all purpose flour
1 cup brown flour
1 tablespoon ghee*
½ teaspoon salt
1 to 2 cups of boiling water

*Ghee is clarified butter.

METHOD
1 Combine both the flours, salt and ghee, in a bowl and carefully bind the dough with boiling water (use a spoon or fork to bind the dough).
2 Make 1 inch balls and roll out into 4 inch rounds
3 On a hot tava* cook roti on both sides till it puffs up (or till it is cooked).
4 Spread some ghee on hot roti and serve with any curry dish.

*A Tava is a cast iron plate which is heated on a stove. One can use a cast iron frying pan in it's place.

SPICY PURI

INGREDIENTS

2 cups all purpose flour
2 teaspoon ginger/garlic masala
½ teaspoon green chillie masala
½ teaspoon red chillie powder
¼ teaspoon turmeric powder
1 teaspoon salt
3 tablespoons oil
1 to 2 cups warm water
4 cups of oil (to deep fry)

METHOD

1 Combine flour, ginger/garlic masala, green chillie masala, red chillie powder, turmeric, salt and 3 tablespoons of oil. Bind dough with warm water to the consistency of a bread dough.

2 Form 1 inch round balls and roll out into 2 inch rounds with a rolling pin.

3 Deep fry in hot oil, till golden brown.

4 Once cooled store in an airtight container.

Makes about 3 dozen.

A great snack!

Sweet Puri

INGREDIENTS

2 cups all purpose flour
1 tablespoon sugar
½ teaspoon salt
2 tablespoons corn oil
¼ cup ghee (clarified butter)
1 tablespoon sesame seeds
1 to 2 cups of water
4 cups of oil (to deep fry)

METHOD

1 Combine all the ingredients with water to make a soft dough.
2 Take a handful of dough and roll out like a pizza.
3 Spread ghee on the dough. Sprinkle flour lightly over top.
4 Roll up the dough like a swiss roll and cut into half inch slices.
5 Roll out the slices into small 2 inch rounds and deep fry in hot oil till golden brown.
6 Store in an airtight container when cooled.

Makes about 3 dozen.

FOOLECHA

INGREDIENTS

3 cups all purpose flour
**4 teaspoons crushed cumin
seeds**
1½ teaspoons salt
2 tablespoons fast active yeast
2 teaspoon sugar
4 tablespoons olive oil
1 to 2 cups of hot water
4 cups of oil (to deep fry)

Foolecha can be served with any of the
spicy dishes, especially meat curries.

METHOD

1 Mix flour, cumin seeds, salt,
yeast, sugar and oil, till the flour
is crumbly.

2 Bind the dough with hot water
and let the dough rise for about
2 hours. Cover the dough with a
cloth.

3 Take a handful of dough and roll
out like a pizza to about ¼ inch
thick.

4 Cut out with cookie cutter and
deep fry till golden brown. (Any
shape cookie cutter can be
used.)

NAAN OR PITA BREAD

INGREDIENTS

3 cups all purpose flour

3 teaspoons crushed cumin seeds

1½ teaspoons salt

2 tablespoons fast active yeast

1 teaspoon sugar

2 tablespoons corn oil

1 to 2 cups of hot water

METHOD

1 Using all the ingredients, bind the dough the same way as the foolecha and let it rise for 2 hours.

2 Make 2 inch round balls. Roll into oblong shapes of ¼ inch thick and cook on a hot tava* on medium heat.

3 Cook on both sides. Naan will puff up.

4 Butter both inside and out with some butter.

Naan can be served with any of the spicy dishes, especially meat curries.

*Tava is a concave pan used for cooking Indian breads.

Daksha's Herb Bread

Serves six

INGREDIENTS

1 loaf of French bread
3 garlic cloves
¼ cup chopped fresh cilantro
½ teaspoon salt
3 teaspoons crushed cumin
5 tablespoons soft butter or margarine

METHOD

1 Grate the garlic finely or put through a garlic press.
2 Mix cilantro, salt, garlic, and cumin with the soft butter or margarine.
3 Cut the bread in ½ to ¾ inch slices (not all the way through). Spread both sides of the slices, lightly, with the butter mixture.
4 Wrap the bread in a tin foil. Bake in a preheated oven of 350°F for 50 minutes (or bake on a barbecue at medium heat for 40 minutes).

BASMATI RICE

INGREDIENTS

1 cup of basmati rice
1 teaspoon salt
2 cups of water
1 tablespoon ghee (clarified butter)

METHOD

1 Wash rice in water about 3 times or till water is clear.
2 Cook rice in a pot with 2 cups of water, on medium heat.
3 Cook for about 10 to 15 minutes or till rice is half cooked.
4 Drain rice in a small holed colander.
5 In a separate pot add the drained rice and ¼ cup of water. Spread ghee over the rice. Cover and allow to cook on low heat for about 15 to 20 minutes or till rice is fully cooked.

Notes

Condiments Masalas & Desserts

Notes

Spicy Tomato Sauce

INGREDIENTS

1 cup ketchup
3 tablespoons vinegar
1 or 2 grated garlic cloves
½ teaspoon red chillie powder
1 teaspoon ground cumin
¼ teaspoon mustard powder
½ teaspoon salt

METHOD

1 Mix all the ingredients in a bowl and chill before serving.
2 Store in refrigerator. Great with barbecues, roast potatoes, samosas and also good as a dip.

Cilantro Chutney

INGREDIENTS

3 bunches of cilantro
2 green chillies
3 garlic cloves
½ teaspoon pickling salt
2 teaspoons whole cumin seeds
juice of half a lemon

METHOD

1 Wash and drain cilantro in a colander.
2 Process all the ingredients together in a chopper till smooth.
3 Add juice of half a lemon before serving. Store in a refrigerator.

Great with any meat dish or barbecues.

GINGER/GARLIC MASALA

INGREDIENTS

1 cup of garlic peeled
1 cup of ginger peeled
3 or 4 green chillies
½ teaspoon pickling salt

METHOD

1 Peel and wash garlic and ginger. Wash chillies.
2 Blend in a chopper or blender till finely chopped and store in sealed container in the freezer.

GREEN CHILLIE MASALA

INGREDIENTS

1 cup of green chillies
¼ teaspoon pickling salt

METHOD

1 Wash and drain green chillies
2 Blend green chillies with salt in a chopper or blender till finely chopped. Store in sealed container in the freezer.

GARLIC MASALA

Garlic masala is blended in the same way as the green chillie masala, with the same amount of salt to a cup of peeled garlic and 2 to 3 green chillies. Again store in a sealed container in the freezer.

COOL MELON DESSERT

Serves eight to ten

INGREDIENTS

½ a watermelon

½ a cantaloupe

½ a honeydew melon

2 cups of seedless grapes (green and red)

2 tablespoons honey

2 tablespoons lemon juice

6 tablespoons chopped mint

METHOD

1 Remove seeds from all melons.
2 Scoop out into round balls and place in a large dessert dish.
3 Add washed grapes
4 Mix honey, lemon juice and mint in a separate bowl.
5 Pour over all the fruit and blend gently with a spoon.
6 Refrigerate before serving.

A great way to cool your palate and to end a delicious spicy meal!

Raas Malai

INGREDIENTS

500g of Ricotta cheese
1¼ cups of sugar
1½ liters of half and half cream
1 teaspoon vanilla
¼ teaspoon ground cardamom
½ cup thinly sliced almonds
1 tablespoon coarsely ground pistachio nuts

METHOD

1. Mix together ricotta cheese and ¼ cup sugar.
2. Spread mixture on cookie sheet and bake at 300°F for 45-50 minutes. This will dry out all the moisture from the mixture.
3. In a large heavy pot mix together half and half cream, 1 cup sugar, vanilla and ground cardamom. Bring to a boil on medium heat stirring occasionally.
4. Allow baked ricotta cheese to cool, then crumble into a serving dish.
5. Pour the heated cream mixture over the ricotta cheese. Sprinkle almonds and pistachio nuts.
6. Allow to cool and chill.

Raas Malai tastes it's best when chilled.

SEERO

INGREDIENTS

1 cup cream of wheat
4 tablespoons ghee
2 tablespoons sugar
¼ cup raisins
¼ cup chopped almonds
1 cup hot water
1 cup milk
½ teaspoon ground cardamom

METHOD

1 Braise cream of wheat in a heated pot with ghee, on medium heat, until golden brown.

2 Add hot water and milk and stir. Cover and cook for 15 minutes, stirring occasionally.

3 Add sugar, raisins, almonds and cardamom and stir. Cook covered on low heat for another 10 minutes or until the ghee separates. Stir frequently to avoid sticking.

SEV

INGREDIENTS

2 rounds nests of Italian pasta*
4 tablespoons ghee
2 tablespoons sugar
¼ cup raisins
¼ cup chopped almonds
2 cups of hot water
½ teaspoon ground cardamom

*** this comes packaged in thin
nests of pasta strands.**

METHOD

1 Break up the nests of pasta rounds in a pot of hot ghee and braise till golden brown.

2 Add hot water and cook, covered on medium heat for 15 minutes.

3 Add sugar, raisins, almonds and cardamom and allow to cook on low heat. Stir frequently until ghee separates.

Index

Spicy Appetizer Dishes	7
Spicy Tea (Chai)	9
Spicy Meat Balls	10
Samosas	11, 12, 13, 14
Moothya (Spicy Patties)	15
Vadas	16
Patarya (Spicy Spinach Rolls)	17
Potato Snacks	18
Bhajyas (Pakodas)	19
Dokra (Steamed Lentil Cake)	20
Pan Roasted Potatoes	21
Measurements	22
Spicy Meat Poultry & Fish Dishes	**23**
Chicken Pilaf	25
Chicken Curry	26
Bhabuti	27
Spicy Fried Fish	28
Shrimp Curry	29
Spicy Roasted Chicken	30
Tandoori Chicken	31

Index

Spicy Barbecues	**33**
Barbecued Salmon in Lettuce Leaf	35
Barbecued Chicken Kabobs	36
Barbecued Meat Balls	37
Barbecued Spicy Roast Chicken	38
Spicy Barbecued Chicken Pieces	39
Spicy Vegetable Dishes	**41**
Eggplant & Potato Curry	43
Peas & Potato Curry	44
Spicy Corn	45
Spicy Potatoes	46
Spicy Pepper & Potato Dish	47
Spicy Lentil Dishes	**49**
About Lentils	50
Vadhu (Sprouted Mung Curry)	51
Urad Toower Daal	52
Mung Daal	53
Mung Curry	54
Zucchini with Chana Daal	55
Black Eye Bean Curry	56
Toower Daal	57

Index

Indian Breads	**59**
Chappati or Roti	61
Spicy Puri	62
Sweet Puri	63
Foolecha	64
Naan or Pita Bread	65
Daksha's Herb Bread	66
Basmati Rice	67
Condiments, Masalas & Desserts	**69**
Spicy Tomato Sauce	71
Cilantro Chutney	71
Ginger/Garlic Masala	72
Green Chillie Masala	72
Garlic Masala	72
Cool Melon Dessert	73
Raas Malai	74
Seero	75
Sev	76

All the spices and cookware that are use in our
recipes are available at:
Daksha's Gourmet Spices

To Order
Visit our website at
www.spicesgourmet.com